Contents

Introduction. 2

Freeform Methods 2

Motif Patterns 4

Freeform Handbag. 10

Freeform Mesh Jacket. 11

Drawstring Handbag 16

Trefoil Hat 18

Not-So-Victorian Collar. 20

Freeform Triple Treat 22

Abbreviations and Stitch Symbols 31

Introduction

In the 1970s, there was a movement toward a form of crochet that has become known as Freeform Crochet. Freeformers did not want to follow patterns; they liked to do their own thing. Some did a whole garment in one piece, randomly using different yarns and different stitches. One of the methods from that era was the making of many smaller pieces from many yarns and stitches, much like the pioneers. The small pieces were then combined into a garment that became a one-of-a-kind artwork.

Traditional Irish crochet is believed to be the original freeform crochet method. The beautiful leaves and flowers, joined with lovely mesh stitches and Clones knots, worked in tiny stitches and fine cotton, were works of art worn by royalty and the very wealthy.

Two of the early movers and shakers of the freeform movement, James Walters and Sylvia Cosh, coined a word for the small pieces used in making a freeform garment; they named them "scrumbles." Freeform crochet, by some definitions, is a combination of stitches and colors, worked in a multidirectional way. For years, I did all my freeform crochet in neutral colors, with a variety of highly textured stitches in shades of white, beige, and tan. I loved the look. It was not until much later that I began experimenting with more color. Lately, I have tried using one color in different yarns. I have seen gorgeous examples of freeform, using one yarn, one color, many different stitches. Whatever your preference, don't be afraid to experiment. Freeform crochet is not a weekend project, not meant for instant gratification. Allow yourself the time to experiment, play, and get creative. The results are worth it.

Freeform Methods

MESH METHOD

I use several methods to create freeform crochet. The one I find most resembling Irish Crochet, with less work, is embellishing a mesh background. The jacket on page 11 is worked in a mesh stitch with some puff stitches to imitate Clones Knots. You can wear the jacket without further embellishment. To transform it with freeform crochet, I embellished it with some traditional flowers and leaves from old Irish Crochet patterns.

TEMPLATE METHOD

You can also work freeform crochet using a template, such as a piece of paper cut to the shape of the finished piece. This could also be a commercial sewing pattern. Then place small pieces of crochet (scrumbles), like a puzzle, all over your template and sew them together.

LINING METHOD

Similar to the template method is the lining method. In this case, your template is a piece of lining or other fabric cut to the finished shape of the garment or accessory. The scrumbles are then sewn, or appliquéd, to the fabric. The underlying fabric provides support and you don't have to cover it completely if you don't want to. In essence, the scrumbles can be used like appliqués. I have appliquéd scrumbles to gloves and mittens, sock cuffs, cloth slippers, pillows, and even purchased garments, such as sweatshirts.

A sweatshirt can become the lining for a warm freeform jacket. First, cut off all the ribbing at the neck, cuffs, and bottom. Then cut the sweatshirt down center front, creating a cardigan. Pin your scrumbles in place, working from the top down, then hand-sew them to the sweatshirt and to each other as you work. The result is a fairly heavy, lined jacket.

If you would like a lighter-weight jacket, use the sweatshirt as a template only After pinning your scrumbles in place, sew them to each other, but not to the sweatshirt. The sweatshirt can then be removed, and you will have a lovely shaped garment. Add borders, buttonholes, and edges if you want, or leave as is with asymmetrical edges.

TIP

When pinning your scrumbles to the template or lining, do not be afraid to occasionally overlap pieces, or stretch them a little, to fit in a certain space. Where pieces do not exactly meet, use a small flower or little circle to fill in the space.

BEYOND THE FREEFORM FABRIC

A freeform crochet project isn't finished until you are happy with your results. Surface crochet can be used to "correct" a section that you are not fond of, to connect two adjoining scrumbles, to give some conformity, or to fill in a little space. Surface crochet is working over existing stitches from the right side of the work, picking up a loop and working off as usual. Surface crochet also adds dimension and texture to your work.

Embellishing with beads is fun. Sewing a bead in a flower center, or adding a group of beads to fill in an area adds a bit of whimsy or glamour to your work.

The possibilities are endless. Take the first step with instructions, then let yourself have fun and experiment.

BEYOND THE FREEFORM FABRIC

A freeform crochet project isn't finished until you are happy with your results. Surface crochet can be used to "correct" a section that you are not fond of, to connect two adjoining scrumbles, to give some conformity, or to fill in a little space. Surface crochet is working over existing stitches from the right side of the work, picking up a loop and working off as usual. Surface crochet also adds dimension and texture to your work.

Embellishing with beads is fun. Sewing a bead in a flower center, or adding a group of beads to fill in an area adds a bit of whimsy or glamour to your work.

The possibilities are endless. Take the first step with instructions, then let yourself have fun and experiment.

Motif Patterns

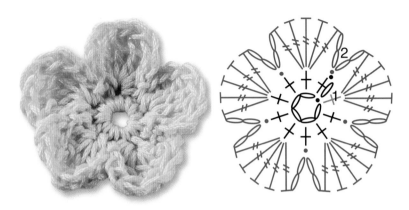

FIVE-PETAL FLOWER

Ch 5, join with a Sl st to form a ring.

Rnd 1: Ch 1, 10 sc in ring, join with a Sl st to first sc.

Rnd 2: *Ch 2, 5 tr in next sc, ch 2, Sl st in next st, rep from * 4 times more, end off.

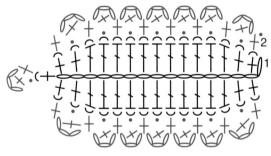

WIDE CURLY EDGED LEAF

Picot: Ch 3, sc in 3rd ch from hook.

Chain 16.

Row 1: 1 sc in 2nd chain from hook, 1 sc in next ch, 1 dc in each of the next 12 chs, 1 sc in next ch, 3 scs in the last chain. Working across opposite side of foundation ch, 1 sc in next ch, 1 dc in each of next 12 chs, 1 sc in each of last 2 chs. Do join, do not turn.

Row 2: Continue working in a spiral, working in the back loop of sts, *sc in the next st [picot, Sl st in next st, sc in next st] 7 times (7 picots)*, [sc in next st, picot, Sl st] in next st (point of leaf made). Working on other side of leaf, rep from * to * across, sl st in next st, fasten off.

IRISH ROSE

Ch 8, join with a Sl st to form a ring.

Rnd 1: Ch 5 (counts as a dc, ch 2), *1 dc in ring, ch 2, rep from * 6 times more, join with a Sl st to 3rd ch of beg ch (8 ch-2 spaces).

Rnd 2: [1 sc, 3 dc, 1 sc] in each ch-2 space around, join with Sl st to first sc (8 small petals).

Rnd 3: Ch 1 (counts as first sc), *ch 5, working behind petals, work 1 sc in first sc of next petal, rep from * 7 times omitting last sc, join with Sl st to beg ch (8 ch-5 loops).

Rnd 4: [1 sc, 1 hdc, 3 dc, 1 hdc, 1 sc] in each ch-5 loop around, join with a Sl st to first sc (8 medium petals).

Rnd 5: Ch 1 (counts as first sc), *ch 7, working behind petals, work 1 sc in first sc of next petal, rep from * 7 times omitting last sc, join with a Sl st to beg ch (8 ch 7 loops).

FANCY SHAMROCK

Ch 6, join with a Sl st to form a ring.

Rnd 1: Work 18 sc in ring, join with Sl st to first sc.

Rnd 2: Ch 1 (counts as first sc now and throughout), skip first sc, 1 sc in each sc around, join with Sl st to beg ch-1.

Rnd 3: Ch 1, skip first ch, 1 sc in each of next 5 sc, [ch 10, 1 sc in each of next 6] twice, ch 12, join with Sl st to beg ch-1.

Rnd 4: Ch 1, skip first ch, 1 sc in each of next 4 sc, [22 sc in next ch-10 space, 1 sc in each next 5 sc] twice, 24 sc next ch-12 space, join with Sl st to beg ch-1.

Rnd 5: Ch 1, sc in next 4 sc *[ch 4, skip 2 sc, sl st in next sc] 7 times, sc in next 5 sc] twice [ch 4, skip 2 sc, sl st in next sc] 8 times, join with a sl st to beg ch-1.

Rnd 6: Ch 1, skip next sc, 1 sc in next sc, [5 sc in next ch-4 space] 7 times, skip next 2 sc, Sl st in next sc, ch 18 for stem, 1 sc in 3rd ch from hook, 1 sc in each of next 15 ch, Sl st in next sc on main motif, [5 sc in next ch-4 space] 7 times, skip next 2 sc, 1 sc in next sc, skip next 2 sc, [5 sc in next ch-4 space] 8 times, join with a Sl st in first sc, end off.

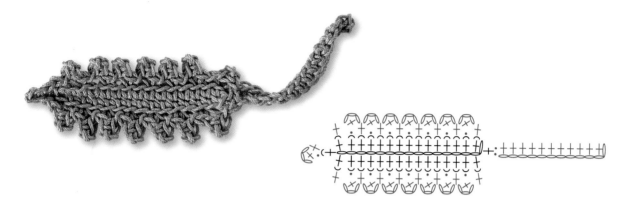

CURLY EDGED LEAF

Picot: Ch 3, sc in 3rd ch from hook.

Chain 16.

Row 1: 1 sc in 2nd chain from hook, 1 sc in next ch, 1 dc in each of the next 12 chs, 1 sc in next ch, 3 scs in the last chain. Working across opposite side of foundation ch, 1 sc in next ch,

1 dc in each of next 12 chs, 1 sc in each of last 2 chs. Do join, do not turn.

Row 2: Continue working in a spiral, working in the back loop of sts, *sc in the next st [picot, Sl st in next st, sc in next st] 7 times (7 picots)*, [sc in next st, picot, Sl st] in next st (point of leaf made). Working on other side of leaf, rep from * to * across, sl st in next st, fasten off.

SMALL LEAF

Note: Work leaf on both sides of the foundation chain.

Ch 12.

Row 1: 5 dc in the 4th ch from hook, 1 dc in each of next 4 ch, 1 hdc in each of next 2 ch, 1 sc in next ch, [sc, ch3, sc] in last ch [point of leaf]. Working across opposite side of foundation ch, 1 sc in next ch, 1 hdc in each of next 2 ch, 1 dc in each of next 4 ch, 5 dc in next ch, ch 3, Sl st in same st as last dc, end off.

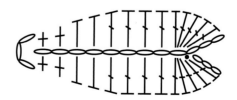

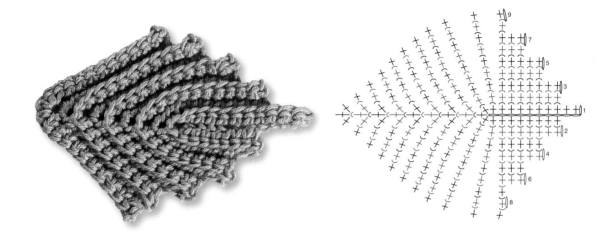

RIDGED LEAF

Notes: When working the ridged leaf, do not count the turning ch 1 as the first st;, when turning, do not skip the first st. Starting with Row 2, work sts in back loops throughout.

Ch 11.

Row 1: 1 sc in 2nd ch from hook, 1 sc in next 8 ch, 5 sc in last ch. Working across opposite side of foundation ch, 1 sc in each of next 7 ch, turn.

Row 2: Ch 1, 1 sc in each of first 9 sc, 3 sc in next sc, 1 sc in next 9 sc, turn.

Row 3: Ch 1, 1 sc in each of first 10 sc, 3 sc in next sc, 1 sc in next 8 sc, turn.

Row 4: Ch 1, 1 sc in each of next 9 sc, 3 sc next sc, 1 sc in next 9 sc, turn.

Row 5: Ch 1, 1 sc in each of next 10 sc, 3 sc in next sc, 1 sc next 8 sc, turn.

Row 6: Ch 1, 1 sc in each of next 9 sc, 3 sc in next sc, 1 sc next 9 sc, turn.

Row 7: Ch 1, 1 sc in each of next 10 sc, 3 sc in next sc, 1 sc next 8 sc, turn.

Row 8: Ch 1, 1 sc in each of next 9 sc, 3 sc in next sc, 1 sc next 9 sc, turn.

Row 9: Ch 1, 1 sc in each of next 10 sc, 3 sc in next sc, 1 sc next 10 sc, end off.

Ch 6, join with a Sl st to form a ring.

BUTTERFLY

Skill Level: Easy

Ch 15, join with a Sl st to the first ch (forming a large loop), ch 15, join with a Sl st in the same st as you joined the first loop (you now have 2 loops), ch 10, join with a Sl st in the same st as other loops are joined, ch 10, join with a Sl st in the same st as other loops are joined (2 ch-15 loops and 2 ch-10 loops).

Rnd 1: Ch 1, [5 sc, ch 4, 1 sc, ch 6, 1 sc, ch 8, 1 sc, ch 10, 1 sc, ch 8, 1 sc, ch 6, 1 sc, ch 4, 5 sc] in each of next 2 ch-15 loops, [2 sc, ch 4, 1 sc, ch 6, 1 sc ch 8, 1 sc, ch 6, 1 sc, ch 4, 2 sc], in each of next 2 ch-10 loops, join with Sl st to beg sc, end off, leaving a 12" (30.5 cm) length of yarn, wrap this around center to form body of butterfly, tie a knot underneath body.

BROAD LEAF

Skill Level: Easy

Note: *Work leaf on both sides of the foundation chain.*

Ch 14.

First half of leaf: 5 tr in 5th ch from hook, 1 tr in each of the next 3 ch, 1 dc in each of the next 2 ch, 1 hdc in each of the next 2 ch, 1 sc in next ch, 1 Sl st in last ch, ch 3, Sl st in the same ch (point of leaf), do not turn.

Second half of leaf: Working across opposite side of foundation ch, 1 sc in next ch, 1 hdc in each of next 2 ch, 1 dc in each of next 2 ch, 1 tr in each of next 3 ch, 5 tr in last ch, ch 3, Sl st in same ch, end off.

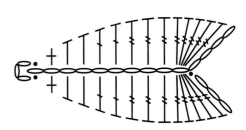

Freeform Handbag

Clutch-style freeform crochet handbags are fun and easy to make, and they are an interesting way to use some of your scrumbles. This bag is made using the lining method of freeforming.

YOU WILL NEED

Scrumbles

⅜ yd (0.35 m) synthetic fleece for interlining

⅜ yd (0.35 m) lining

Needle and thread

Yarn to coordinate with scrumbles

Button

1. Cut interlining to the desired shape. For the handbag shown, cut a 9" × 15" (23 × 38 cm) piece and round one end. Cut a piece of lining, using the interlining as a guide and leaving ½" (1.3 cm) extra on the edge.

2. Arrange the scrumbles on the interlining with their edges touching. Leave as little open space as possible. Open spaces can be filled with additional crochet stitches later. Pin the scrumbles to the interlining.

3. Sew the scrumbles to each other using coordinating lightweight yarn or sew them to the interlining using needle and thread. Fill in any spaces with additional crochet stitches.

4. Work one row sc around entire outside edge. At the center of the rounded end, make a button loop.

5. Place the lining, right side up over the wrong side of the bag piece. Turn under the edge all around so that it just covers the interlining. Pin the lining in place. Stitch the lining to the bag.

6. Fold the bag into an envelope shape and sew the side seams. Add a button. Add a shoulder strap it desired.

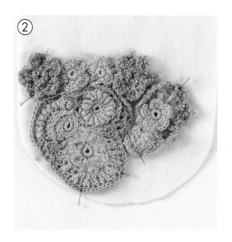

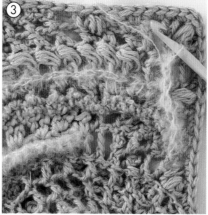

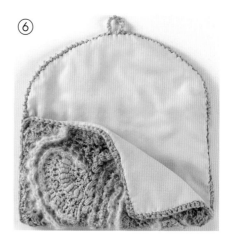

Freeform Mesh Jacket

Follow the directions for the Mesh Jacket (page 12). Then crochet several embellishments from the Motif Patterns Section (pages 4 to 9) and arrange them on the jacket wherever you like. Freeform means following your own muse, so embellish your jacket however you wish. The following instructions detail how I embellished my jacket.

EMBELLISHMENTS

Use light weight and medium weight yarns in a variety of textures and fibers.

Crochet the following embellishments, leaving an 18" (45.5 cm) tail of yarn on each embellishment for sewing motif to garment:

1 Butterfly (page 9) in light smooth

10 Flowers (page 4) in light smooth

14 Broad Leaves (page 9) in medium smooth

10 Broad Leaves (page 9) in medium smooth

10 Flowers (page 4) in medium fuzzy

Using photos as guides, pin motifs in place, then sew to both the mesh base and to each other.

YOU WILL NEED

Yarn
Fine alpaca/silk blend about 1,500 yd (1,380 m)

Hook
4/E (3.5 mm) for main body

5/F (3.75 mm) for embellishments

Stitches used
Chain

Double crochet

Puff stitch

Gauge
8 ch-2 spaces and 9 dc = 4" (10 cm); 10 rows = 4" (10 cm) with 4/E hook

Notions
Tapestry needle

Finished size
Small (Medium, Large, X-large)

Finished chest size after blocking: 39" (42", 45", 48") (99 [106.5, 114.5, 122] cm)

Notes: Puff st: [Yo, pick up a loop] 4 times in same space, yo, pull through all 9 loops on hook.

To decrease 1 space in mesh pattern: At beg of row, ch 3 instead of 5, 1 dc in next dc (this eliminates one ch 2 space). At end of row, eliminate last ch 2, work 1 dc in the turning ch.

Back

Ch 134 (140, 146, 152).

Row 1: 1 dc in 8th ch from hook,*ch 2, skip next 2 ch, 1 dc in next ch, rep from * across, turn (43 [45, 47, 49] ch-2 spaces).

Row 2: Ch 5 (counts as dc, ch 2 now and throughout), skip first dc, 1 dc in next dc, [ch 2, 1 dc in next dc] 2, (3, 4, 5) times, 1 puff st in next ch-2 space, ch 1, 1 dc in next dc, *[ch 2, 1 dc in next dc] 5 times, 1 puff st in next ch-2 space, ch 1, 1 dc in next dc, rep from * across, ending with [ch 2, 1 dc in next dc] 2 (3, 4, 5) times, ch 2, 1 dc in 3rd ch of turning ch-5, turn.

Row 3: Ch 5, skip first dc, 1 dc in next dc, [ch 2, 1 dc in next dc] 1 (2, 3, 4) times, *1 puff st in next ch-2 space, ch 1, 1 dc in next dc, ch 2, 1 dc in next dc, 1 puff st in next ch-2 space, ch 1, 1 dc in next dc**, [ch 2, 1 dc in next dc] 3 times, rep from * across, ending last rep at **, [ch 2, 1 dc in next dc] 1 (2, 3, 4) times, ch 2 ,1 dc in 3rd ch of turning ch-5, turn.

Row 4 for size Small only: Ch 5, skip first dc, *1 dc in next dc, 1 puff st in next ch-2 space, ch 1, 1 dc in next dc, ch 2, rep from * across, ending with last dc in 3rd ch of turning ch-5, turn.

Row 4 for size Medium only: Ch 5, skip first dc, 1 dc in next dc, ch 2, *1 dc in next dc, 1 puff st in next ch-2 space, ch 1, 1 dc in next dc, ch 2, rep from * across to within last ch-2 space, 1 dc in next dc, ch 2, 1 dc 3rd ch of turning ch-5, turn.

Row 4 for size Large only: Ch 5, skip first dc, [1 dc in next dc, ch 2] twice, 1 dc in next dc, *1 puff st in next ch-2 space, ch 1, 1 dc in next dc, ch 2, rep from * across to within last 2 ch-2 spaces, [1 dc in next dc, ch 2] twice, 1 dc 3rd ch of turning ch-5, turn.

Row 4 for size X-large only: Ch 5, skip first dc, 1 dc in next dc, ch 2, [1 dc in next dc, ch 2] twice, 1 dc in next dc, *1 puff st in next ch-2 space, ch 1, 1 dc in next dc, ch 2, rep from * across to within last 3 ch-2 spaces, [1 dc in next dc, ch 2] 3 times, 1 dc 3rd ch of turning ch-5, turn.

Row 5: Rep Row 3.

Row 6: Rep Row 2.

Row 7: Ch 5, skip first dc, 1 dc in next dc, *ch 2, 1 dc in next dc, rep from * across, ending with last dc in 3rd ch of turning ch-5, turn.

Rows 8–10: Rep Row 7.

Rows 11–28: Rep Rows 2–10 (twice).

Rows 29–33: Rep Rows 2–6 (4 complete groups of puff st pattern are completed).

Work even in mesh stitch pattern only for 1 (1, 2, 3) more rows until body measures 13½" (13½", 14", 14½") (34.5 [34.5, 35.5, 37] cm) from beg.

Armhole Shaping

Sl st over first 3 (3, 4, 4) ch-2 spaces, ch 3, work mesh pattern as established to within 3 (3, 4, 4) spaces on other side, leave these sts unworked, turn, cont in mesh pattern dec 1 space each side, every row 3 (3, 4, 4) times, then work even on rem sts until armhole measures 7½" (8", 8½", 9") (19 [20.5, 21.5, 23] cm) from beg of armhole shaping.

Neck Shaping

Work in mesh pattern across 7 (8, 9, 10) ch-2 spaces, end off yarn. Skip center 17 (17, 15, 13 ch-2 spaces), rejoin yarn in next dc, ch 5, work in mesh pattern across (7 [8, 9, 10] ch-2 spaces), end off.

Left Front

Ch 62 (68, 74, 80).

Row 1: 1 dc in 8th ch from hook,*ch 2, skip next 2 ch, 1 dc in next ch, rep from * across, turn (19 [21, 23, 25] ch-2 spaces).

Work same as Back to armhole.

Armhole Shaping

Starting at armhole edge, Sl st over first 3 (3, 4, 4) ch-2 spaces, ch 3, work in mesh pattern as established across to end of row, turn, keeping front edge even, cont in pattern as established, dec 1 space each armhole side, every row 3 (3, 4, 4) times.

V Neck Shaping

When armhole dec are completed, work armhole side even and dec 1 space at neck edge every other row until 7 (8, 9, 10) ch-2 spaces rem, work even until armhole measures 8" (8½", 9", 9½"), (20.5 [21.5, 23, 24] cm) end off.

Right Front

Work same as Left Front to armhole.

Armhole Shaping

Starting at neck edge, work across row to within last 3 (3, 4, 4) ch-2 spaces, turn, ch 3, work in mesh pattern as established

to end of row, turn, keeping front edge even, cont in pattern as established, dec 1 space each armhole side, every row 3 (3, 4, 4) times.

V Neck Shaping

When armhole dec are completed, keep arm side even and dec 1 space at neck edge every other row until 7 (8, 9, 10) ch-2 spaces rem, work even till armhole measures 8" (8½", 9", 9½") (20.5 [21.5, 23, 24] cm), end off.

Sleeve (make two)

Ch 80 (86, 92, 98).

Row 1: 1 dc in 8th ch from hook,*ch 2, skip next 2 ch, 1 dc in next ch, rep from * across, turn (25 [27, 29, 31] ch-2 spaces).

Rows 2–10: Work same as Back.

Rows 11–15: Rep Rows 2–6.

Work 1 (1, 2, 3) more rows even.

Cap Shaping

Sl st over first 3 (3, 4, 4) ch-2 spaces, ch 3, work in mesh pattern as established to within 3 (3, 4, 4) spaces on other side, leaving these sts unworked, turn. Cont in mesh pattern, dec 1 space each side, every row 3 (3, 4, 4) times. Work even on rem sts until cap measures 6" (6½", 7", 7½") (15 [16.5, 18, 19] cm) from beg of cap shaping. Dec 1 space each side of next 2 rows, end off.

(continued)

Sleeve Bell Bottom

Same for all sizes, worked in the round.

Sew underarm seam of sleeve.

Rnd 1: With RS facing, join yarn at seam, ch 1, work 70 sc evenly spaced around bottom of sleeve, working the sts in the ch-2 spaces, join with a Sl st to first sc.

Rnd 2: Ch 3 (counts as half a V-st now and throughout), *skip next 2 sc, [2 dc, ch 2, 2 dc] in next sc (shell made), skip next 2 sc, [1 dc, ch 2, 1 dc] in next sc (V-st made), rep from * around end-1 dc in same sc as beg ch 3, ch 2, join to top of beg ch-3, forming last V-st (12 shells, 12 V-sts).

Rnd 3: Ch 3, *[2 dc, ch 2, 2 dc] in center ch-2 space of next shell, V-st in center ch-2 space of next V-st, rep from * around, ending with 1 dc in ch-2 space of last V-st, ch 2, join with a Sl st to top of beg ch-3.

Rnds 4–7: Rep Rnd 3.

Rnds 8–13: Ch 3, *[3 dc, ch 2, 3 dc] in center ch-2 space of next shell, V-st in center ch-2 space of next V-st, rep from * around, ending with 1 dc in ch-2 space of last V-st, ch 2, join with a Sl st to top of beg ch-3.

Rnd 14: Ch 3, 1 dc in same st as ch 3, *[3 dc, ch 3, 3 dc] in center ch-3 sp of next shell, [2 dc, ch 3, 2 dc] in center ch-3 space of next V-st, rep from * around, ending with 2 dc in ch-3 space of last V-st, ch 3, join with a Sl st to top of beg ch 3, end off.

Sweater Edging

Use a tapestry needle to sew shoulder seams.

Row 1: Starting at bottom right front, join yarn, ch 1, work 2 sc in each open space all around front and neck edges to bottom left front corner, turn.

Row 2: Ch 1, skip first sc, 1 sc in each sc across, turn.

Row 3: Ch 1, skip first sc, 1 sc in each sc to beg of V-neck shaping on Right Front, ch 61 for tie, 1 sc in 2nd ch from hook, 1 sc in each ch across, 1 sc in each sc across neck edge to bottom of V-neck shaping on Left Front, ch 61 for tie, 1 sc in 2nd ch from hook, 1 sc in each ch across, 1 sc in each sc across to bottom of Left Front, do not turn, cont in sc along bottom edge, working 2 sc in each ch-2 space, join with a Sl st in first sc at bottom of Right Front, end off.

Finishing

Pin Sleeves in place centering on shoulder seam and matching underarm seams, sew in place.

Blocking

Lay garment flat on a towel-padded surface, spritz lightly with water, and pat into shape. Do not iron or press flat; allow to thoroughly dry.

Drawstring Handbag

Everyone needs a special-occasion handbag! Crochet a number of these drawstring purses in varying colors so you can shift bags with the seasons. Got a wedding coming up? Make the bag in white as a gift for the bride.

Skill Level: Experienced

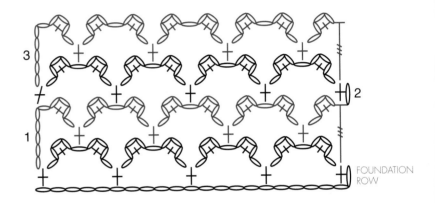

Notes: Bag is made in one piece, folded, and sewn at sides. Lining and embellishments are added before sewing. Double Triple Crochet (dtr): Yo 3 times, [yo, draw through 2 loops on hook] 4 times.

The space in the center of the double picot is where you will be making the scs.

PICOT MESH BASE

Chain 37

Foundation Row: 1 sc in 2nd ch from hook, *[ch 4, 1 sc in 3rd ch from hook (picot made)] twice (double picot made), ch 1, skip next 4 ch, 1 sc in next ch, rep from * across, turn.

Row 1: Ch 9, (counts as 1 dtr, ch 4), 1 sc in 3rd ch from hook (picot), ch 1, sc in space in the center of the next double picot, *[ch 4, 1 sc in 3rd ch from hook] twice, ch 1, 1 sc in the space in the center of the next double picot, rep from * across, ch 4, 1 sc in 3rd ch from hook, 1 dtr in last sc, turn.

Row 2: Ch 1, 1 sc in first dtr, *[ch 4, 1 sc in 3rd ch from hook] twice, ch 1, 1 sc in space in the center of the next double picot, rep from * across, ending with last sc in the 5th ch of the beg ch 9, turn.

Rep Rows 1 and 2 for 30 rows, ending with row 1.

To finish, work as follows: ch1, *sc in next picot, ch2, rep from * across row, end with 1 sc in last sc.

Motifs
Make 3 Five-Petal Flowers (page 4).

Make 1 Fancy Shamrock on (page 6).

Make 4 Wide Curly Edged Leaves (page 4).

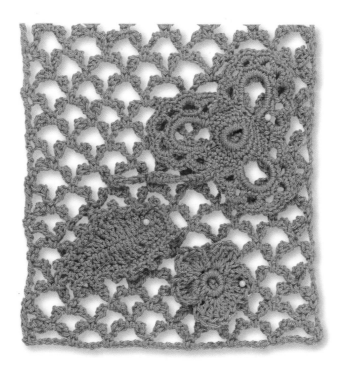

Finishing

When pieces are all finished, pin the base piece on a padded surface to measure 7 1/2" × 18" (19 × 45.5 cm). Sprinkle with water, pat into shape, and allow to dry. When dry, pin embellishments in place and sew onto mesh.

Lining

Cut two pieces 8½" × 19" (21.5 × 48.5 cm), sew three sides together, leaving one short end open, and turn inside out so seams are on the outside. (The inside of the lining bag will be finished.) Turn ½" (1.3 cm) of the open side of the lining to the outside, sew it to WS of one side of the top of the bag. Fold the bag, and repeat, sewing the lining to the other side of the bag. With bag folded in half around lining, sew side seams of bag, using a simple weaving stitch.

Top Border: Join yarn at a side seam. Working along top edge of bag, work in rnds.

Rnd 1: Ch 1, 3 sc in each ch space all around top of bag, join with sl st to beg ch-1. Do not turn.

Rnd 2: (Beading Row): Ch 5 (counts as a dc, ch-2), *sk 1 sc, 1 dc in next sc, ch 2, rep from * around, join with sl st to 3rd ch of beg ch-5.

Rnd 3: Ch 1, 2 sc in each ch-2 sp around, join with a sl st to beg ch-1.

Rnd 4: Ch 1, 1 sc in first sc, *ch 4, 1 sc in 4th ch from hook (Picot made), sk 1 sc, 1 sc in next sc, rep from * around, join with sl st to beg sc. Fasten off.

Tie (make two)

Using double strand of yarn, ch 125. End off. Weave ties in and out of beading row. Start one tie on one side and start the second tie on the opposite side, weaving the ties in opposite directions. Securely knot ends of each tie together; sew over knot using a needle and thread. Arrange the ties so that knots will be hidden in Rnd 2 at top edge of bag, leaving the ties neatly finished.

Trefoil Hat

Caps off to handsome headwear! Use Irish Crochet motifs in unusual ways to make one-of-a-kind wearables. Here, I used a very common Trefoil motif to create an exceptional beret.

Skill Level: Experienced

YOU WILL NEED

Yarn

Lightweight cotton yarn, 270 yd (250 m)

Hook

F/5 (3.75 mm)

6/G (4.00 mm)

Gauge

7 dc with ch 2 in between = 4" (10 cm) on 6/G hook.

Finished size

21" (53.3 cm) head size (To make larger size, omit decreases on Rnd 22, work the rnd even, then complete band on 90 stitches instead of 80.)

Notes: Beret is started in center top, with F/5 hook, worked in rnds down toward band.

Picot: ch 3, sl st into first ch of 3 chs just made.

BERET

Rnd 1: Ch 10, sl st in first ch to form a loop, [ch 9, sl st into same ch as last sl st] twice. (3 loops formed)

Rnd 2: * Ch 1, working into next ch-9 loop, work [2 sc, 1 hdc, 11 dc, 1 hdc, 2 sc], ch 1 sl st into same ch as sl st of first rnd, rep from * twice more.

Rnd 3: Sl st into each of first 9 sts of first loop [ch 16, sk 8 sts of first loop, sk first 8 sts on next loop, sl st into next dc] twice, ch 16, sl st into same dc as last sl st at beg of rnd. (3 ch-16 loops)

Rnd 4: Ch 1, work 1 sc into same dc as last sl st of previous rnd, work 19 sc into the first ch-16 loop [1 sc into same dc as next sl st of previous rnd, 19 sc into next ch-16 loop] twice, sl st into first sc. (60 sc)

Rnd 5: Ch 8 (counts as 1 dc plus ch-5) skip next 3 sc, [1 dc into next sc, ch 5, sk 3 sc] 14 times, sl st into 3rd ch of the beg ch-8. (15 ch-5 loops)

Rnd 6: Sl st into first 3 ch of the first ch-5 loop, ch 1, 4 sc into the first loop, 7 sc into each of the next fourteen ch-5 loops, 3 sc into same loop as the first 4 sc, sl st into the first sc. (105 sc)

Rnd 7: [Ch 6, sk next 6 sc, sc into next sc] 14 times, ch 6, sl st into same sc as last sl st of previous rnd. (15 ch-6 loops)

Rnd 8: Sl st over 4 ch, ch 1 (counts as sc), 4 sc in first loop, * 9 sc in each of the next 14 loops, end 4 sc in same loop with beg 4 sc, sl st to beg ch-1. (135 sc)

Rnd 9: *Ch 9, sk 8 sc, sc in next sc, rep from * around, join with a sl st to base of beg ch-9. (15 ch-9 loops)

Rnd 10: Rep Rnd 8.

Rnd 11: Rep Rnd 9.

Rnd 12: Rep Rnd 8.

Rnd 13: *Ch 5, sk 4 sc, 1 sc in next sc, ch 5, sk 3 sc, 1 sc in next sc, rep from * ending ch 5, join with a sl st to base of beg ch-5. (30 ch-5 loops)

Rnd 14: Change to 6/G hook, ch 1, 5 sc in each ch-5 loop, join with a sl st to first sc. (150 sc)

Rnd 15: Ch 5 (counts as 1 dc, ch-2), *sk 2 sc, 1 dc in next sc, ch 2, rep from * around, join with a sl st to 3rd ch of beg ch-5. (50 ch-2 loops)

Rnd 16: Ch 6 (counts as 1 dc, ch-3), *1 dc in next dc, ch 3, rep from * around, join with a sl st to 3rd ch of beg ch-6. (50 ch-3 loops)

Rnd 17: Ch 7 (counts as 1 dc, ch-4), *1 dc in next dc, ch 4, rep from * around, join with a sl st to 3rd ch of beg ch-7. (50 ch-4 loops)

Rnd 18: Ch 8 (counts as 1 dc, ch-5),*1 dc in next dc, ch 5, rep from * around, join with a sl st to 3rd ch of beg ch-8. (50 ch-5 loops)

Rnd 19: Ch 1, 3 sc in each ch-5 loop around, join with a sl st to beg ch-1. (150 sc)

Rnd 20: Ch 1, *1 sc in each of the next 2 sc, sk next sc, rep from * around, join with a sl st to beg ch-1. (100 sc)

Rnd 21: Ch 1, *1 sc in each of the next 8 sc, sc2tog, rep from * around, join with a sl st to beg ch-1.(90 sc)

Rnd 22: Ch 1, *1 sc in each of the next 7 sc, sc2tog, rep from * around, join with a sl st to beg ch-1.(80 sc)

Rnds 23, 24, 25: Ch 1, 1 sc in each sc around, join with a sl st to beg ch-1.

Rnd 26: Work 1 Rnd of reverse sc, fasten off.

Not-So-Victorian Collar

Perk-up a little black dress or energize a lackluster top with a delicate lacy collar that you crocheted using a fine cotton yarn. This project may challenge your skills, but you'll find the flattery-evoking accessory well worth your efforts.

Skill Level: Experienced

YOU WILL NEED

Yarn
Superfine cotton, 225 yd (206 m)

Hook
B/1 (2.5 mm)

Gauge
1 motif = 2" (5 cm) wide
Motifs are worked in rnds.

BASE MOTIF

Ch 7, join with a sl st to form a ring.

Rnd 1: Ch 6 (counts as 1 dc, ch 3), 1 dc in ring, [ch 3, dc in ring] 6 times, ch 3, join with sl st to 3rd ch of beg ch-6 (8 ch-3 spaces).

Rnd 2: Ch 1, [1 sc, 3 dc, 1 sc] in each ch-3 space around, do not join.

Rnd 3: [Sl st from the back around post of next dc of Rnd 1, ch 6] 8 times, do not join (8 ch-6 loops).

Rnd 4: [1 sc, 1 hdc, 5 dc, 1 hdc, 1 sc] in each ch-6 loop around, join with sl st to first sc. Fasten off.

SECOND MOTIF

Rep Rnds 1 through 3 of Base Motif, then join to Base Motif as follows: in ch-6 loop work [1 sc, 1 hdc, 2 dc, sl st to center dc of any petal of Base Motif, continue 3 dc, 1 hdc, 1 sc] in same lp on motif in progress, make [1 sc, 1 hdc, 2 dc in next ch-6 loop, join to center st of next petal on base motif, make 3 dc, 1 hdc, 1 sc] in same loop (petals joined). Finish as Base Motif.

Continue in this manner, making new motifs and joining new motifs always on Rnd 4, following photo for placement.

FREEFORM CROPPED VEST **FREEFORM LONG VEST** **FREEFORM JACKET**

Freeform Triple Treat

Here are three different designs made from one pattern—a cropped vest, a long vest, and a jacket all crocheted in the same lighter-than-air cashmere/silk blend yarn. Using several different size hooks creates the shaping, so there is very little increasing and decreasing. The neck and armhole shaping is the same for all garments; if you would like a scoop neck, just leave as is; if you would like a V neck, turn back the front edges to create the V. Want to customize the design? Add embellishments that reflect your personality.

Skill Level: Intermediate

Note: When working sl st over stitches at armhole or neck edges, make 3 sl sts in each loop, 1 sl st in each sc, 1 sl st in each dc. Pattern stitch is multiple of 8 plus 6.

Double Triple Crochet (dr): Yo 3 times [yo, draw through 2 loops on hook] 4 times.

The space in the center of the double picot is where you will be making the scs.

MAYA MESH

Ch a multiple of 8 plus 6.

Foundation Row: 1 sc in 2nd ch from hook, 1 sc in each ch across row, turn.

Row 1: Ch 1, sc in first sc, *ch 5, skip next 3 sc, 1 sc in next sc, rep from * across, turn.

Row 2: Ch 3 (counts as first dc), 3 dc in next ch-5 loop, *ch 3, 1 sc in next ch-5 loop, ch 3, 3 dc in next ch-5 loop, rep from * across to last ch-5 loop, 1 dc in last sc, turn.

Row 3: Ch 1, 1 sc in first st, *ch 5, 1 sc in next ch-3 loop, rep from * across, ending with last sc in top of turning ch, turn.

Row 4: Ch 6 (counts as dc, ch 3), 1 sc in next ch-5 loop, *ch 3, 3 dc in next ch-5 loop, ch 3, 1 sc in next ch-5 loop, rep from * across to last ch-5 loop, ch 3, 1 dc in last sc, turn.

Row 5: Ch 1, 1 sc in first st, ch 5, skip first ch-3 loop, 1 sc in next ch-3 loop, *ch 5, 1 sc next ch-3 loop, rep from * across, ending with last sc in 3rd ch of turning ch, turn.

Rep Rows 2–5 for pattern.

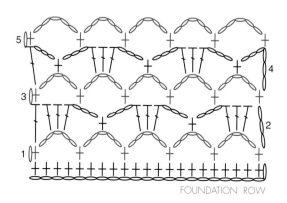

FOUNDATION ROW

YOU WILL NEED

Yarn

Superfine cashmere/silk blend. (1,650 yd (1,500 m) for long vest); 990 yd (910 m) for cropped vest; 1,320 yd (1,215 m) for cardigan

Hooks

D/3 (3.25 mm), E/4 (3.5 mm), F/5 (3.75 mm), and G/6 (4 mm) for long vest

D/3 (3.25 mm) and E/4 (3.5 mm) for cropped vest

C/2 (2.75 mm), D/3 (3.25 mm), and E/4 (3.5 mm) for cardigan

Gauge

To check your gauge, using E/4 (3.5 mm) hook, ch 30, work pattern for 16 rows. Piece should measure 4" × 4" (10 × 10 cm)

Notions

Tapestry needle

Matching thread

Finished Sizes

Small (Med, Large, X large)

Finished chest size (after blocking) 34 (36, 38, 40)" (86.3 [91.4, 96.5, 101.6] cm)

FREE-FORM CROPPED VEST

Back

With E/4 (3.5 mm) hook, ch 118 (126, 134, 142), work Maya Mesh Pattern (page 24) until 7" (18 cm) from the beg, ending with Row 4 of pattern.

Armhole Shaping

Sl st over 8 (10, 12, 14) sts, continue with Row 5, omitting 8 (10, 12, 14) sts at other side. Change to D/3 (3.25 mm) hook and continue in pattern as established till 8½ (9, 9½, 10)" (21.5 [22.8, 24.1, 25.4] cm) from armhole. Fasten off.

Left Front

Ch 54 (62, 70, 78), work same as back to armhole, ending with Row 4 of pattern. Sl st over 8 (10, 12, 14) sts, continue pattern to end of row. Change to D/3 (3.25 mm) hook, continue pattern as established until armhole is 7" (18 cm), ending at arm edge with Row 3.

Shape Neck

Continue with Row 4, omitting last 24 (24, 26, 28) sts, work same as Back to shoulder on rem loops. Fasten off.

Right Front

Repeat Left Front to armhole, ending with Row 4 of pattern, work across row, omitting last 8 (10, 12, 14) sts, turn. Continue pattern as established until same as Left Front to Neck Shaping, ending with Row 4 at neck edge, sl st over 24 (24, 26, 28) sts, continue pattern as established on rem loops until same as Back to shoulder.

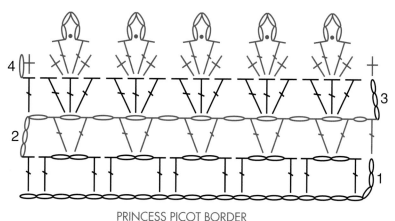

PRINCESS PICOT BORDER

Embellishments
With E/4 (3.5 mm) hook, make nine Five-Petal Flowers (page 4), three Ridged Leaves (page 8), and one Irish Rose (page 5).

Finishing
Sew shoulder and side seams.

Bottom Border
With RS facing, with E/4 (3.5 mm) hook, work Princess Picot Border as follows.

Row 1: 1 dc in 4th ch from hook, *ch 2, skip next 2 ch, 1 dc in each of next 2 ch, rep from * across, turn.

Row 2: Ch 4 (counts as dc, ch 1), *[1 dc, ch 1, 1 dc] in next ch-2 space (V st made), ch 1, rep from * across, 1 dc in top of turning ch, turn.

Row 3: Ch 3 (counts as first dc), *skip next ch-1 space, 3 dc in ch-1 space of next V st, rep from * across, 1 dc in 3rd ch of turning ch, turn.

Row 4: Ch 1, 1 sc in first dc, *, [1 sc, 1 dc, ch 4, Sl st in 4th ch from hook (picot made), 1 dc, 1 sc] in center dc of next 3-dc group, rep from * across, 1 sc in top of turning ch, end off.

With E/4 (3.5 mm) hook, work 1 row sc all around front and neck edges. Pin embellishments on as shown in photo and sew in place.

Ties (Make two)
Cut two, 2½ yd lengths (2.2 m) of yarn. Fold both strands through edge loop on one side of front, following placement in picture. Holding all four strands together, work ch until end. End off, securing with tight knot, and cutting ends to about ¼" (6 mm). Rep for other side.

Blocking: Lay garment on a padded surface, sprinkle with water, pat into shape, and allow to dry.

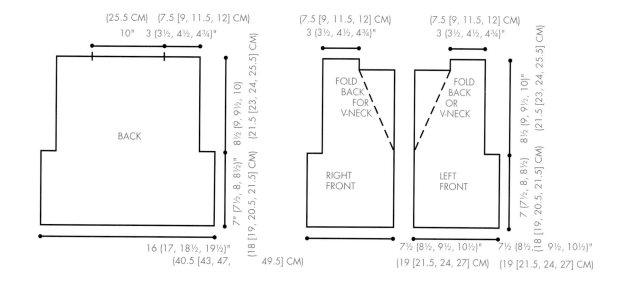

Back

With G/6 (4 mm) hook, ch 118 (126, 134, 142), work Maya Mesh Pattern (page 23) till 12 (12, 12½, 12½)" (30.4 [30.4, 31.7, 31.7] cm) from beg. Change to F/5 (3.75 mm) hook, continue pattern for 12" (30.4 cm) more, change to E/4 (3.5 mm) hook, continue pattern until 30 (30, 30½, 30½)" (76.2 [76.2, 77.4, 77.4] cm) from beg, ending with Row 4 of pattern.

Armhole Shaping

Sl st over 8 (10, 12, 14) sts, continue with Row 5, omitting 8 (10, 12, 14) sts at other side. Change to D/3 (3.25 mm) hook and continue in pattern as established until 8 (8½, 9, 9½)" (20.3 [21.5, 22.8, 24.1] cm) from armhole, fasten off.

Left Front

Ch 54 (62, 70, 78). Work same as back to armhole, ending with Row 4 of pattern. Sl st over 8 (10, 12, 14) sts, continue pattern to end of row. Change to D/3 (3.25 mm) hook, continue in pattern as established until armhole is 6½ (7, 7½, 8)" (16.5 [17.7, 19, 20.3] cm), ending at arm edge with Row 3.

Shape Neck

Continue with Row 4, omitting last 24 (24, 26, 28) sts, work same as Back to shoulder on rem loops. Fasten off.

Right Front

Work same as Left Front to armhole, ending with Row 4 of pattern. Work across row omitting last 8 (10, 12, 14) sts, turn. Continue pattern as established until same as Left Front to Neck Shaping, ending with Row 4 at neck edge, turn, sl st over 24 (24, 26, 28) sts, continue pattern as established on rem loops till same as Back to shoulder.

Embellishments

With E/4 (3.5 mm) hook make six Five-Petal Flowers (page 4), nine Ridged Leaves (page 8), and one Irish Rose (page 5).

Finishing

Sew shoulder and side seams, leaving 12 (12, 12½, 12½)" (30.4 [30.4, 31.7, 31.7] cm) from bottom open for slit.

Bottom Border

With RS facing, use E/4 (3.5 mm) hook, work Princess Picot border (page 25) on back and fronts. Using E/4 (3.5 mm) hook, work 1 row sc all around front and neck edges. Pin embellishments on as shown in photo; sew in place.

Ties (Make two)

Cut two, 2½ yd lengths (2.2 m) of yarn. Fold both strands through edge loop on one side of front, following placement in picture. Holding all four strands together, work ch until end. End off, securing with tight knot, and cutting ends to about ¼" (6 mm). Rep for other side.

Finishing

Blocking: Lay garment on a padded surface, sprinkle with water, pat into shape, and allow to dry.

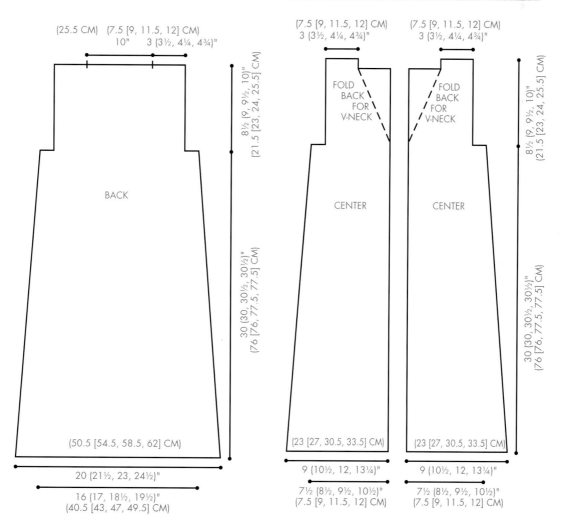

(25.5 CM) (7.5 [9, 11.5, 12] CM)
10" 3 (3½, 4¼, 4¾)"

8½ (9, 9½, 10]"
(21.5 [23, 24, 25.5] CM)

BACK

30 (30, 30½, 30½]"
(76 [76, 77.5, 77.5] CM)

(50.5 [54.5, 58.5, 62] CM)
20 (21½, 23, 24½)"

16 (17, 18½, 19½)"
(40.5 [43, 47, 49.5] CM)

(7.5 [9, 11.5, 12] CM)
3 (3½, 4¼, 4¾)"

(7.5 [9, 11.5, 12] CM)
3 (3½, 4¼, 4¾)"

FOLD BACK FOR V-NECK

CENTER

FOLD BACK FOR V-NECK

CENTER

8½ (9, 9½, 10]"
(21.5 [23, 24, 25.5] CM)

30 (30, 30½, 30½]"
(76 [76, 77.5, 77.5] CM)

(23 [27, 30.5, 33.5] CM)
9 (10½, 12, 13¼)"

7½ (8½, 9½, 10½)"
(7.5 [9, 11.5, 12] CM)

(23 [27, 30.5, 33.5] CM)
9 (10½, 12, 13¼)"

7½ (8½, 9½, 10½)"
(7.5 [9, 11.5, 12] CM)

FREEFORM JACKET

Back

With E/4 (3.5 mm), ch 118 (126, 134, 142), work Maya Mesh pattern (page 23) till 11 (11½, 12, 12½)" (27.9 [29.2, 30.4, 31.7] cm) from beg, ending with Row 4 of pattern.

Armhole Shaping

Sl st over 8 (10, 12, 14) sts, continue with Row 5, omitting 8 (10, 12, 14) sts at other side. Change to D/3 (3.25 mm) hook and continue in pattern as established till 8 (8½, 9, 9½)" (20.3 [21.5, 22.8, 24.1] cm) from armhole. Fasten off.

Left Front

Ch 54 (62, 70, 78). Work same as Back to armhole, ending with Row 4 of pattern. Sl st over 8 (10, 12, 14) sts, continue in pattern to end of row. Change to D/3 (3.25 mm) hook. Continue in pattern as established until armhole is 6½ (7, 7½, 8)" (16.5 [17.7, 19, 20.3] cm), ending at arm edge with Row 3.

Shape Neck

Continue with Row 4, omitting last 24 (24, 26, 28) sts. Work same as back to shoulder on rem loops. Fasten off.

Right Front

Work same as Left Front to armhole, ending with Row 4 of patt. Work across row omitting last 8 (10, 12, 14) sts, turn. Continue pattern as established until same as Left Front to Neck Shaping, ending with Row 4 at neck edge. Turn, sl st over 24 (24, 26, 28) sts, continue pattern as established on rem loops till same as back to shoulder.

Sleeves

With C/2 (2.75 mm) hook, ch 70 (70, 78, 86). Work Pattern Rows 1–5, then rep Pattern Rows 2–5, four times more, change to D/3 (3.25 mm) hook, continue to rep Pattern Rows 2–5 till 18 more Pattern Rows completed. Change to E/4 (3.5 mm) hook, continue in pattern until 16 (16, 18, 18) more rows completed.

Shape Cap

Sl st over 8 (10, 12, 14) sts, continue in pattern as established omitting last 8, (10, 12, 14) sts. Change to D/3 (3.25 mm) hook, continue in pattern for 7 more rows, change to C/2 (2.75 mm) hook and work pattern for 6 (8, 10, 12) more rows. Fasten off.

Embellishments

Use E/4 (3.5 mm) hook, work three Five-Petal Flowers (page 4), nine Ridged Leaves (page 8), and one Irish Rose (page 5).

Finishing

Sew shoulder and side seams.

Bottom Border

With RS facing, using E/4 (3.5 mm) hook, work Princess Picot border (page 25). Using E/4 (3.5 mm) hook, work 1 row sc all around front and neck edges. Pin embellishments on as shown in photo; sew in place.

Ties (Make two)

Cut two, 2½ yd (2.2 mm) lengths of yarn. Fold both strands through edge loop on one side of front, following placement in picture. Holding all four strands together, work ch until end. End off, securing with tight knot, and cutting ends to about ¼" (6 mm). Rep for other side.

Finishing

Blocking: Lay garment on a padded surface, sprinkle with water, pat into shape, and allow to dry.

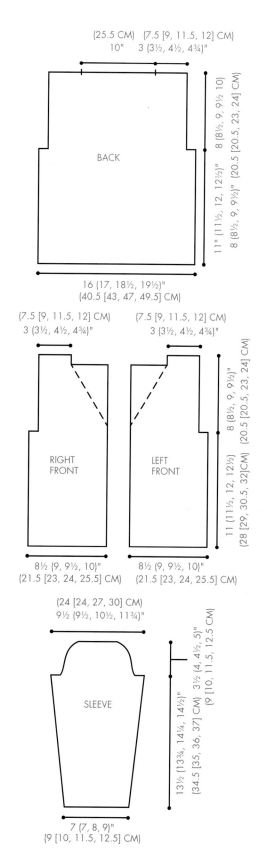

Abbreviations & Stitch Symbols

approx	approximately	FPdc	front post double crochet	sk	skip
beg	begin/beginning			SI st	slip stitch
bet	between	FPsc	front post single crochet	sp(s)	space(s)
BL	back loop(s)			st(s)	stitch(es)
bo	bobble	FPtr	front post triple crochet	tbl	through back loop(s)
BPdc	back post double crochet	g	gram(s)	tch	turning chain
		hdc	half double crochet	tfl	through front loop(s)
BPsc	back post single crochet	inc	increase/increases/increasing	tog	together
				tr	triple crochet
BPtr	back post triple crochet	lp(s	loop(s)	trtr	triple triple crochet
CC	contrasting color	Lsc	long single crochet	tr2tog	triple crochet 2 together
ch	chain	m	meter(s)		
ch-	refers to chain or space previously made e.g., ch-1 space	MC	main color	TSS	Tunisian simple stitch
		mm	millimeter(s)	WS	wrong side(s)
		oz	ounce(s)	yd	yard(s)
ch lp	chain loop	p	picot	yo	yarn over
ch-sp	chain space	patt	pattern	yoh	yarn over hook
CL	cluster(s)	pc	popcorn	[]	Work instructions within brackets as many times as directed
cm	centimeter(s)	pm	place marker		
cont	continue	prev	previous		
dc	double crochet	qutr	quadruple triple crochet	*	Repeat instructions following the single asterisk as directed
dc2tog	double crochet 2 stitches together	rem	remain/remaining		
dec	decrease/decreases/decreasing	rep	repeat(s)	**	Repeat instructions between asterisks as many times as directed or repeated from a given set of instructions
dtr	double treble	rev sc	reverse single crochet		
FL	front loop(s)	md(s)	round(s)		
foll	follow/follows/following	RS	right side(s)		
FP	front post	sc	single crochet		
		sc2tog	single crochet 2 stitches together		

TERM CONVERSIONS

Crochet techniques are the same universally, and everyone uses the same terms. However, US patterns and UK patterns are different because the terms denote different stitches. Here is a conversion chart to explain the differences.

US	UK
single crochet (sc)	double crochet (dc)
half double crochet (hdc)	half treble (htr)
double crochet (dc)	treble (tr)
triple crochet (tr)	double treble (dtr)

CROCHET DIAGRAM SYMBOLS

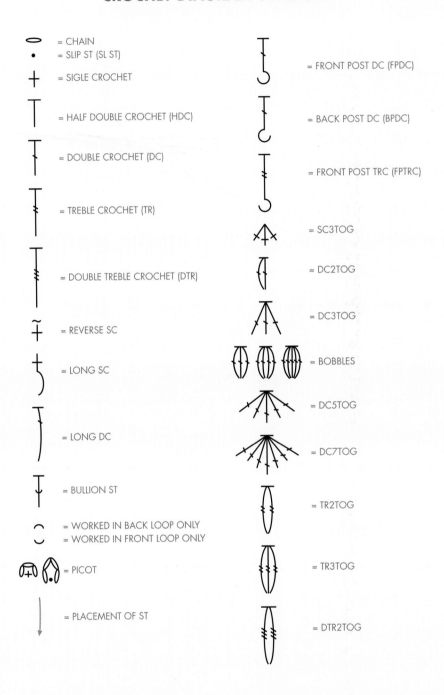

= CHAIN

= SLIP ST (SL ST)

= SIGLE CROCHET

= HALF DOUBLE CROCHET (HDC)

= DOUBLE CROCHET (DC)

= TREBLE CROCHET (TR)

= DOUBLE TREBLE CROCHET (DTR)

= REVERSE SC

= LONG SC

= LONG DC

= BULLION ST

= WORKED IN BACK LOOP ONLY
= WORKED IN FRONT LOOP ONLY

= PICOT

= PLACEMENT OF ST

= FRONT POST DC (FPDC)

= BACK POST DC (BPDC)

= FRONT POST TRC (FPTRC)

= SC3TOG

= DC2TOG

= DC3TOG

= BOBBLES

= DC5TOG

= DC7TOG

= TR2TOG

= TR3TOG

= DTR2TOG